Dear Reader,

Thank you for purchasing this book! This book was created out of my desire to teach children and adults that the Bible contains answers for all of life's questions. I am praying that this book is a blessing to you.

To learn more about me or to download free resources for this book, please visit my website www.booksbycorine.com. You can also contact me there. I love hearing from my readers.

As always, please pray for me and know that I am praying for you,

Corine

Dedication
May all the glory and honor
go to the Savior and Lord of the world,
Jesus Christ.

Scripture quotations marked (NIV) are taken from the New International Version (NIV). Copyright © 1973, 1978, 1984, 2011 by Biblica.

Teaching Christ's Children
Baltimore, Maryland

http://www.TeachingChristsChildren.com

What is Love?

A Kid Friendly Interpretation of 1 John
3:11, 16-18 & 1 Corinthians 13:1-8 & 13

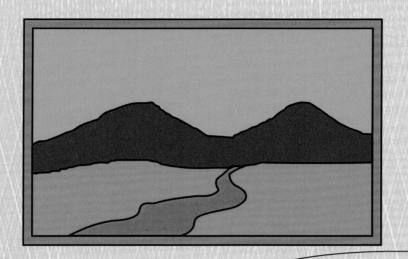

We just finished learning what the Bible has to say about love. We would like to share what we learned with you.

The first thing we learned is very simple. You should definitely start with this: love each other.

† For this is the message you heard from the beginning: We should love one another. 1 John 3:11.

You may be wondering what exactly is "love?" The Bible tells us we know what love is because He loves us so much He died for us.

✝ *This is how we know what love is: Jesus Christ laid down his life for us. And we ought to lay down our lives for our brothers and sisters. 1 John 3:16*

Let's say we are very, very rich. We see someone who needs something but don't help. Do we really love God? No, of course not.

✝ *If anyone has material possessions and sees a brother or sister in need but has no pity on them, how can the love of God be in that person? 1 John 3:17*

Or how about if I spoke every language in the world and could sing like an angel, but I didn't love...

† *If I speak in the tongues of men or of angels, but do not have love, 1 Corinthians 13:1a*

Then no one would want to listen to me.

✝ *I am only a resounding gong or a clanging cymbal. 1 Corinthians 13:1b*

Or if I had so much faith, I could do impossible things like make mountains disappear.

✝ *And if I have a faith that can move mountains.*
1 Corinthians 13:2b

But if we don't love others, it would mean nothing.

† *But do not have love, I am nothing.*
1 Corinthians 13:2c

Love is waiting patiently and is always kind.

† *Love is patient, love is kind.*
                    1 Corinthians 13:4a

When I love, I don't want what others have. Nor do I brag about what I have.

†*It does not envy, it does not boast, it is not proud.*
1 Corinthians 13:4b

When I love, I don't get easily angered and I don't remember the bad things others do.

✝ *It is not easily angered; it keeps no record of wrongs. 1 Corinthians 13:5b*

Because I love, I don't like it when I sin.

✝ *Love does not delight in evil.*
   1 Corinthians 13:6a

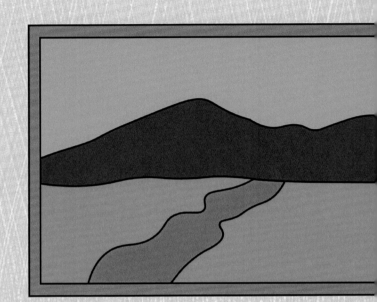

Because I love, I am happy when I know the truth, even when I'm told I was wrong.

✝ *But rejoices with the truth.*
1 Corinthians 13:6b

Because I love, I take care of people.

We will always have three things in life, faith, hope and love. But love is the best.

✝ *And now these three remain: faith, hope and love. But the greatest of these is love. 1 Corinthians 13:13*

1 John 3: 11, 16-18

11 For this is the message you heard from the beginning: We should love one another. 16 This is how we know what love is: Jesus Christ laid down his life for us. And we ought to lay down our lives for our brothers and sisters. 17 If anyone has material possessions and sees a brother or sister in need but has no pity on them, how can the love of God be in that person? 18 Dear children, let us not love with words or speech but with actions and in truth.

1 Corinthians 13:1-8a & 13

13 If I speak in the tongues of men or of angels, but do not have love, I am only a resounding gong or a clanging cymbal. 2 If I have the gift of prophecy and can fathom all mysteries and all knowledge, and if I have a faith that can move mountains, but do not have love, I am nothing. 3 If I give all I possess to the poor and give over my body to hardship that I may boast, but do not have love, I gain nothing.

4 Love is patient, love is kind. It does not envy, it does not boast, it is not proud. 5 It does not dishonor others, it is not self-seeking, it is not easily angered, it keeps no record of wrongs. 6 Love does not delight in evil but rejoices with the truth. 7 It always protects, always trusts, always hopes, always perseveres.

8 Love never fails. 13 And now these three remain: faith, hope and love. But the greatest of these is love.